Love Story

A compilation of Channeled Poetry to Activate Divine Union

POUPLISHED BY: Veronica Parks

This book is available in print and digital formats.

ISBN: 978-1-968682-05-7 (digital)

ISBN: 978-1-968682-02-6 (print)

Cover design by Veronica Parks

Published by Channeling Evolution

First edition

Printed in USA

Table of Contents

Preface

Welcome beautiful Soul
To this moment in time
When we get to Ignite
The Evolution of Heart

This Book is a gathering
Of Channeled Poetry Codes
Given to me by the Source
To Activate Divine Unions

These are Codes to Awaken
The God love, within your Heart
To Rise in Love with you
And Align with the One

Read from the beginning
Until the very end

To integrate the initiation
Of your Divine Union Path

Read it a few times
Until you Receive no more
Until your Heart is Open
To Love the God IN you

Think of this, as an Activation
Of the memory IN your DNA
It is not a simple Book
It is an initiation of New Earth

My Heart Goes out to you
May this assist you on your Rise
You will find even more jewels
On the "Channeling Evolution" path

https://channelingevolution.com/join

Chapter 1 – Choose Love

Reclaim Yourself

Call back your power
To Love with no limitation
To Love with no condition
Or judgement of Creation

Call back your essence
Loving all that you are
The elixir of Divinity
You are a Superstar

Call back your Voice
To speak your highest truth
To share the loving words
Of what you choose to live

Call back your right to choose
What feels good to you
The true Heart Desire
Your inner child will Love you

Call back your right
To take space IN the world
To BE all that you came to BE
Returning the judgment to all

Call back your Vision
To Create your own Dream
To make the impossible possible
To inspire the rest within

Call back your right
To have freedom of thought
To Connect Heart to mind
And become the One

Call back your Temple

To BE at Peace inside

To BE safe in your wholeness

To BE at home IN Heart

Heart Whisper

A whisper of the Heart
We hear with much Passion
A longing for something
A feeling of Expansion

A whisper from the Soul
To listen to the Heart
A dream and signs appear
To See this new expression

The Heart whisper becomes a voice
A longing for something more
For a true Connection
That feels right to the Soul

The whisper becomes a shout
The Desire IN your Heart

Will inspire the unthinkable
BE ready for it at last!!!

The whisper of the Heart
Gave you time to prepare
Answer the instinct
Before it makes you Aware

The whisper of the Heart
To Align with what brings you Joy
To what turns your Kundalini on
What is your heart longing for?

The whisper of the Heart
Now becomes a Call
No longer listening to the Voice
Of the ego mind

The whisper is what drives you
Into the Magical world

To Feel Love in all beings
Even those who fight it off

The whisper is a Calling
To Love the whole World
How can you limit
A Love that has no end?

The elixir of Creation
As you taste the Expansion
Shows you that Love is alive
Once more IN all Creation!!!

Taste Of Love

The Ecstasy of the moment
When you are touched by Love
Butterflies all over!!!
The world is sheer sky

Oh, what a Sensation
You Feel that you can fly
The whole world as you know it
Stops, in that moment IN time...

You become One
Enveloped in Present
So, in Love with life
Touched by Heaven

A touch that makes you tremble
Every cell shivering with heat

The heart is beating faster, and faster
Yet, nothing has been moved externally

A simple touch charged with energy
Love electricity enveloping the mind
Losing control...
A touch of ecstasy to BE One with all

No time.
No space.
Not thoughts.
Pure Bliss of pleasure
Of a loving embrace

The impulse to live big!!!
To BE Awake and ecstatic
For the world to mirror
The Pleasure within

Chapter 2 - Love Story Begins

Love Story

For this Love story to begin
The old must BE forgiven
Clearing the emotional charge
Of those who came before

We let go of what was
What doesn't fit our purpose
We let go of the fear
Attached to old trajectory

For the Love story to begin
We must commence all new
As if we were Rising in Love
For the first time too!!!

For the Love story to begin
We must BE fully Here
Reclaiming all thoughts
From what was before

For the Love story to begin
We must clear the slate clean
We let go of items and memories
That don't belong IN our Dream

We let it all go...
The bad and the good
We Open to Rise in love
With whom we were meant to

We Open to Receive
The One aligned in Destiny
The One igniting
Every cell IN our body

To shout "You are mine and I am yours
Ready to begin this Love Story
What was, doesn't come with me
I Am Ready"!!!

Ancestors Love

Ancestors are calling
For us to Connect
To unlock the mystery
Of Love IN our DNA

Our Ancestors have gifts
Ancient ways to Honor each other
As we set the stage for this Love story
We Awaken our Lineage to stand by it

This will BE a Union
Of those who came before
From our Ancestral DNA
And the One we rise in Love with

Our lineages will Unite
If they choose too
Our Love will BE as strong
As the bond between the two

A Divine union doesn't stand a chance
Without all members Aligning
Clearing the karma from our DNA
To make the Union possible

This is the call
To say "Yes" to Ancestral lineage
They bow before you
To express their welcome home

As we clear karmic contracts
For all Ancestors of our lineage
In return they will support us
IN every possible way

They will Activate gifts
Residing IN our DNA
For every karma we end
A gift will unlock to See the way

Now, we begin to See how
There is no skipping this process
This transmutation is needed
To form a Divine Union this day

So, when we are ready
We forgive all that was...
All that has been wronged before
We transmute into Love and Light for all

We clear all blocks and resistance
Between the two Ancestor lineages
We say "Yes", and it shall BE
We are complete here

Now, before we go
We Unite both Lineages
And raise their Harmony
So, they can help us in Union

We will BE fully supported
By two powerful lineages
Now, we are ready
To form a Divine Union

The Ancestors blessings
Have been gifted to us
We Receive with Gratitude
Heaven on Earth is here!!!

Imagine Your Partner

The Love story we Create
IN our Vision, with what feels great
Fueled with emotions that we are loved
By us, and the Mirror we seek outside

We begin to Imagine
That exciting Feeling
Of becoming One
With another being!

We imagine the other person
Being an extension of us
Whatever we Feel now
They can Sense it too

Our problems become theirs
And vice versa for us
Imagine our mirror
Uniting with us

You say, “What mirror?
I’m not looking for me
I’m looking for something
That is opposite than me”

Yes and no, as we come to believe
That mirror shows us parts we like
And parts we Choose to hide
They could BE the same or opposite

A Perfect Creation
IN the making
Imagine wisely
This Love Awaking

Imagine being that being
That you wish to Unite with
Imagine how you can Bloom into
The person you Choose to commit

Imagine both sides
How can you Expand?
The Love story to inspire
The entire World at hand

Imagine being that Lover
That you wish to commit
Becoming the best version
That you came to BE!!!

https://channelingevolution.com/join

Chapter 3 - Before You Know

Falling IN Love

When we fall IN Love
We are allowing another
To carry the weight
Or fill a void needed to BE filled

When we fall IN Love
We can lose ourselves IN the process
Fitting IN a piece of their puzzle
Saying Yes to conditional Love

Instead, we Rise IN Love
So, we, plus the other
Can become bigger
Than the sum of two

We Rise in Love because we want
To help the other person Bloom
Who they already are
Because we truly Love them

They will Rise in Love too
To inspire us to BE
Even Happier than we are
And mirror our greatness to See

Not because we are missing something
And we need to fall IN Love
For another to catch us,
But because we are Love

Rise in Love beautiful Soul
As you See each other grow
You will inspire each other BE
The best version that you See

Love You

Love you and all that you are
Love on the good parts
And the ones you hide
That is what true Love is
Accepting all that you are

Love you first
Before you expect that in another
Love all that was and receive
All lessons it thought you

Love your wins
And especially your failures
Love that you had resilience
To BE Reborn a Warrior

Love what you didn't
Love what you couldn't
Love that you forgot
You co-created the riddle

Love the Love itself
Because that is the Bridge
That Unites us all
IN a full Community

Love is the liquid gold
To your way back home
To the Heaven within
A Heart of God to Feel

Open Heart

Open Heart is the Key
To all our dreams and desires
When we Love fully, doors Open
The key is our Loving Heart to BE

We Open our Heart to infinity
To Love a stranger like a brother
Only several generations ago
We were probably brothers

Every person coming into our life
Is related to the same journey
They might BE from our past self
Our Present, or future Dream to See

We Open our Heart to truly Feel
That through the frequency of Love
Everything lies before our eyes
To unfold like a Masterpiece

We Open our Heart
To unlock the biggest treasure
The Golden Key to all our dreams
Is awakening as we Choose Love to See

https://channelingevolution.com/join

Chapter 4 - Ignite The Flame

First Kiss

You tuned into the Love frequency
Manifesting your perfect match
You begin to Feel the longing
The energy of the first Kiss

Oh, you can only Imagine
The heat of the discovery within
When something is taking over
And you become One in Dream

The whole world stops, in that moment
As if you were in another dimension
Bathing IN the frequency of Love
You Experience the full immersion

The touch, the heat, the sensation
The curiosity of something big
The Heart is pounding faster
The body shouting Yes within

I want to taste you, I want to Feel you
What is like to BE with you
Sharing the frequency of entering
The Garden of Eden IN you

A Kiss that will seal Eternity
Of two Souls embraced in Love
A promise of a true Home
Of a Love you dreamed before

What is like?
To taste the Energy within
To BE embraced IN a Dance
Of two Souls Uniting in dream

The Sensation and the shiver
Of the Desire within
Every cell Activating the magnet
To taste what you See IN them

You trust the Feeling
You don’t really have a choice
You have already said, Yes
To experience the first Kiss

The touch, the Sensation
The lips Connecting two Souls
The same channels that guide
This entire world to BE

This is what Creation feels like
Beyond the mind control
It is the Godly energy
Of two longing Souls

The attraction to another
That pulls you IN so strong
With an Eternal Kiss
You Open a whole new world

A world of two Souls Connecting
For the third energy to BE born
The Union Power will unfold
The gift of the Eternal Soul

That is what we came here for
The first Kiss creating
An Opening,
To a New World!

Ignite Union

This Union of two Souls to BE
Is a Creation of the future society
A new generation of Light beings
To rebuild Atlantis

This Divine Union will generate
A 5th dimensional way of being
You are reading the book
Of this New Society

A Union between two souls
IN Love with all they are
A pure co Creation
Of the God we are

The Union will Activate
The Divine Matrix, for all to upgrade
You will upgrade to the frequency of Love
As you become inspired by it!

Divine Union will BE the norm
IN the New Earth creations
The 3D relationships won't hold
These Divine Union high vibrations

Prepare for the Divine Union
This is the Salvation you seek
The God codes will Awaken
As you Unite within

The Union begins inside
Between your masculine and feminine
As you unite within, you magnetize Union
IN the perceived Reality to BE

Union Codes

This Love will unlock
The next level of Codes
To set up the stage
For the New Earth

It will change your body
To Connect as One
It will tune your vessel
For telepathic Communication

You will Feel a Bond
Like no other before
As if they are a true Extension
Of your physical existence

The communication will begin
Before you form the Union
You will prepare each other
To stand this strong Union

Your body is upgrading
To the level of your DNA
Your Heart is Expanding
To receive this Love again

Preparation will amplify
As you get close to Union
Your dreams will become vivid
You will Sense reunion

Your gifts will come online
Feeling jolts of inspiration
To Express fully
And ignite connection

Chapter 5 - Codes of Creation

Creation Codes

The codes of Creation
As they come to BE
Will integrate a new level of Divinity
IN what we consider relationships

A Union based on trust
On connection to a Higher Purpose
A call of two Hearts to Unite
And Create the New World

The discernment for what Love is
Will Awaken as you read this
The longing for your match
Will heighten your ability

He will feel IN his DNA
When he sees her
She will know true home
When she hears him

They will know IN an instant
When they are both ready
For this Divine Union
To materialize Heaven

A Union that will shift
The world as we know it
Into a new way of being
The One you only dreamed of

You found the other part of the coin
The Yin and Yen to form a Union
The foundation of the New Earth
True Creation of Love beings

The rest will follow
When they are ready
You, take the first step
Creating the Bridge for Humanity

Taste co-Creation

You can taste the co Creation
As you made space to BE
IN Love with the idea
Of a Divine Union to See

Allow yourself to Dream
This dream into creation
Feel the ecstasy of uniting
To God IN co Creation

This Divine Union
Will unlock New Codes
The orgasmic sensation
Of Heaven on Earth

Feel the Sensation
Of what is coming to BE
A true Union of hearts
Formed IN Divinity

You are Opening up
Like a Lotus Flower
To Receive this Love
A true Union Power

You will BE met
With your own greatness
You will Rise IN Love
With their whole beingness

Your partner has dreamed
Your very presence IN reality
As you have considered
A parallel reality

Taste the sensation
Of being One with you
A completion of the longing
Of a true soul Union to BE

Taste the co-Creation
And magnetize to you
The being you dreamed into reality
That is a perfect match for you

Activate co-Creation

The codes of co Creation
Are being Activated now
You will feel the sensation
Of your burning Heart

The rain clears all that was
Purifies the water from before
It sets the new Creation
Into pure Manifestation

The stage is clear to Align
The two hearts longing to Love
To Create something more
Bigger than they imagined before

The path is Open to Connect
The energy of fear dissipates
You remember that Love
Is what you came for
To continue Evolution

https://channelingevolution.com/join

Chapter 6 - Activate Union

Create Love Story

The Love story you Create
It's more than you anticipate
When Aligned with another Soul
You are changing history as we know

This Love will BE noticed
And analyzed by all
It will BE an INerstanding
Of a higher level of growth

The words as you speak today
Will BE used with caution
You will communicate
Very Telepathically

You will know each other's needs
You will Feel each other's hearts
You will thrive to improve
On this Creation inside

Your Union will show the way
To find your true Divinity
When your bodies Align
You will form a Trinity

That is the union of two souls
On all time frames and dimensions
And the Divine IN you
As to form the trinity

The new earth codes download to See
What Heaven on Earth is like
IN full Unity with the partner
You are Aligned to Create Trinity

Love Story Awaken

This Love Story will remind you
The intensity of the past
The frustration of not having
What you are feeling now

Your Love story will Awaken
Years of longing life
How could you have missed it?
How could you have forgot?

This Love, you only dreamed of
Someone that knows you at heart
A Heart you longed for lifetimes
A kiss you climbed mountains for

This Love will Awaken
Dormant DNA Codes in you
You will Receive inheritance
From those who came before you

Your Love will Advance
The new Humanity to come
This Love is the base
For the 2nd Messiah to Rise

Your Love will Awaken the world
You will merge as One
A story to BE shared
For generations to come

This Love has been Prophesized
That will neutralize every war
This Love will Unite all nations
This is the Love you longed for

Activated Love

You Activated the Love
You are ready to Receive
The intensity is real
It will open everything

All the parts you hid
All the parts you left behind
All that you consider good or bad
This person will Love all of it

This will shock you to the core
That they can See through you
Their version of Perfection
That they Feel for you

You will Feel the same
The qualities and difference
It will Open up your Heart
To see the whole Beingness

This Activation will shift you to the core
Even before you meet the other
So, you can Receive the Codes
Immersing with intensity

https://channelingevolution.com/join

Chapter 7 - And so, it Begins

Kundalini

Kundalini Energy
Is the heat of Love to BE
It will envelope your entire body
It will shed all constriction to See

Kundalini energy will Awaken you
Before your partner can come close
You become familiar with this energy
You learn how to Channel it

Kundalini Energy
Is a Divine power Source
Hidden by the patriarchy
Because of the secret it holds

When Kundalini is Awakened
And you experience the energy stream
Of sexual flow with no guilt and restriction
Or projections of the world to hear

This pure energy will Flow
Connecting you to your destiny
Awaken the Kundalini power
It is your Divine right to Feel

When two Awakened Souls
Embrace their Kundalini Energy
And come together as a force
Nothing can stand IN the way

Human Evolution becomes the way
This secret is the very One
That has been shamed in every way
By religion, dogmas and society
Deemed unworthy of Divinity

The very sexual Energy
That birthed us into reality
This is the 1st distorted program
Of disowning our true self

Embrace the Kundalini energy
Allow it to Awaken the fire IN you
Awaken the stream of Sexual Energy
Get to know your body through

Get to know the extreme pleasure
Of you, feeling your body Divine
With the stream of this energy
Simply by being alive

Once you grasp your Kundalini
The stage has already been placed
For the two Activated souls
To come IN full Unity

Divine Union Meeting

A Love like no other
You will meet again
The One written in your Star
Reflected IN your DNA

You are meant to ground a Love
Of a Higher Frequency
A love that will set the base
For the New Earth to BE

This Love Union will defy all odds
It will BE impossible to control
The moment you surrender to it
It will fully unfold and carry you on

You will live Heaven on Earth IN Unity
As together you are forming the trinity
Your Love being supported
By your true Divinity

This Love will inspire many
And it will trigger a few
This love will BE the only way
You begin to See for you

You will notice the illusion
You have lived before
Settling for the confusion
Of the 3D realm

This Love has no boundaries
It is beyond this world
It will defy the very logic
Of all you knew before

The Wait

The wait can BE frustrating
Because you are waiting for you
If you were fully ready
The Union would BE

Simply ask to clear
All that stands in the way
Dissipate the contracts
Residing IN your DNA

Upgrade to the Holy you
The One you came to BE
When you Feel complete
You will remember the Union

The heart belongs to you
To the Godly you
The One that has always
Been there guiding you

Upgrade the old programing
Of the 3D Union
Clearing all debts, karma and pain
Restoring the Holiness of your DNA

https://channelingevolution.com/join

Chapter 8 - Rising Questions

Why Do We Love?

Why do we have we a Heart
To Love with no limitation?
We are advanced species
That can Create on this planet

I invite you to consider
Why given the power of Love?
If sex is all that is needed
For procreation, like other species

Why given the ability to Love?
If we could advance without feelings
I mean, we are creating robots
More Advanced than human beings

Why give us the ability to Love, what for?
What is the riddle of such price
To feel Love and sadness, to feel it all
Why give us Power that we can't control?

A beautiful question inviting an answer
To what is the reason for pain and karma
When we have infinite potential
Beyond any robot created before
We have a Heart to Love, "what for?"

The wisdom coming through
Is that what makes us Godly
Is the ability to circulate pure life force
This infinite Love energy through our body

The Love energy circulating through
Makes everything grow and bloom
Make nations Expand to more
It raises us from primal instinct

To Evolve it all
To Create so much Beauty
To Create a whole New World
We can BE in Harmony with all

The perception is becoming clear
Being advanced beings, here
With the power of God to Love
We can Connect all worlds to Unite

Through Love we are able
To Connect all beings here
Love is the God IN our DNA
To Unite and Create more beings

Once freed from the constriction
We become One with Love
We become limitless beings
The key is IN our Heart

The Mist

The mist of the shadow
You can't See ahead
The mystery seems farther
How could you have missed a turn?

We went through it all and felt the rainbow
Yet, this mist is clouding the vision ahead
How are we supposed to know
If we took the right step?

The doubt begins to creep in
This is the ultimate test
Can we believe IN the Love
We are here to Connect?

This doubt is the last test
Before we know for sure
Before our DNA and Spirit
Has become One in Union

We and our Lover
Are Connecting paths
We are both Rising
To fulfill One mission

Ignore the interfering doubt
This is left over lingering fear
Cut the cord from old stories
And BE fully immersed IN here

Let this rest and integrate
Resume when you are ready
And BE here

Ready For Union

You are ready for Union
You have claimed yourself
You declared your Heart
To loving the Source within

You are ready to receive your lover
The One that matches you in Union
Yin and Yen, dancing between the energies
Of all that you are and can BE

Your telepathic Connection
Will increase as you become
Alike, with each other
Igniting the power of God

The Union is ready
To manifest IN your reality
All will BE Aligned
For this step of your Destiny

Enjoy the moment of now
Before all you know changes
Enjoy this time you have
Don't rush and miss the Present

BE Happy in Union with you
And when you had enough of this Love
Your lover will appear
So, you can both Ascend to the next level

As Yin and Yen in Unity
Your codes are necessary in this weaving
You are ready for Divine Union

https://channelingevolution.com/join

Chapter 9 - Divine Union Heat

Tantric Dream

Have a Tantric Dream
Before you can BE ready
To Feel that with your match
Tasting the intensity of opposite
A passion like no other
Your bodies will roar

Are you ready for such intensity?
It will Feel as if you left the sphere
As if you have been transported
To another dimension of Ecstasy

The intensity of the moment
As the energy is building up
Will Awaken the heat
Of your loving Heart

You will Feel the pull
The power electricity
Of two Godly beings
IN explosion of Energy

Yet, you both became such masters
Of keeping the intensity of pleasure
Under an inner peace expression
You already know this connection
Of push and pull with inertia

The heart and Soul are calling
To touch them and BE One
Yet, the mind, losing control

Turns on the fear at its fullest

Oh, you are both so strong
Life thought you to BE warriors
To endure it all with Grace
Now, you can't control it
And you know this

You have done the work
The Warrior served its part
Let go of controlling the pleasure
And embrace the Heart

One touch of electricity
And all rules are off
Sparks of energy connecting
The Holiest magnetism
You lost control

You no longer belong to you
But to the ecstasy of the moment
Of being One with you
The part you longed to touch you

You have waited for so long
An Embrace that melts all fear
A home that has all that you need
A nourishing Love holding you near

It feels as if Heaven is here
The true embrace of Hearts
You have been dreaming of
Now enjoy the electric Touch

Eternal Love

The petals of this Love story
As it begins to unfold
It envelops you in a tornado
Of Desire and deep longing
To taste the drops of Divine gold

What an intense Desire
To BE One with every touch
With every breath of Ecstasy
Contract, relax, let go of thought

Expand to BE One with all
As you taste the Ecstasy of being
One God, One body, One breath
One drip of infinity...

Feel this IN your body
It holds you so intense
So much Pleasure arising
Can you hold still?

Just a moment longer
Hold this eternal embrace
Of being One with each other
Feel it fully before it happens

Keep the Vision blurry
For the One that is for you
Only with that being
You will Feel this level of Ecstasy

Hold it, hold it still...
Keep unifying the Heat of your fields
The Dragon fire is Awakening your DNA
To another level of pleasure today!!!

How can it BE, is this even Real?
You Feel as if you are One with all
Shivering with Ecstasy
The Explosion is near, can you hold?

Can you hold and...
Send it through your Crown Chakra
So, your beloved can Receive it
The one for you, will Feel it too

This is pure God energy
Share it with your Divine match
Or send it through the Crown chakra
To the Highest you

Enjoy the Eternal Love making
Before it becomes to BE
What you envision and Feel
Will manifest soon for you

These are Codes to Awaken
You, and the ONE for you
Until then, shine your Temple Light

Close the door to your Temple
You are holding pure God gold
Receive this transmission
And BE One with you

Awaken High Heart

Imagine your Heart Expanding
To Love beyond your mind
Beyond the walls of expectation
Beyond what you have ever thought

To Open to such level
Of receiving Godly Love
Imagine every cell of your Heart
Expanding beyond its perceived size

See every cell Opening
Like a Lotus Flower
Igniting in Tantric Love
With all that you are

All that you have been
All that you choose to BE
All you have Connected to

Beyond your limits to See

How could it BE, you ask?
Can I truly expand my heart
Beyond my human mind
Can I Connect right now
With my Godly heart?

You give it a go
As you believe, the God IN you
Imagine Opening your Godly power
To Love beyond your human Heart

Let God penetrate every cell of your Heart
With its loving touch and Pure Light
See yourself Aligning with your High Heart
To BE One with God

https://channelingevolution.com/join

Chapter 10 – Higher INnerstanding

Love IN = IN Love

The Love story begins unfolding
When the Desire for the other cools off
Time comes to stop, you forget to notice
Anything outside of the Loving you

Right IN that moment
You have sent a signal
To Align in Divine Union
Within and with the other

When you realize that you are
Everything you seek and ever wanted
IN that moment, another whole being

Will Awaken to share the world with you

When two Divine hearts Unite
The Magic begins to manifest outside
Sexual energy running through the spine
Ignites pleasure ready to embrace inside

How could it BE
You are all that you seek?
Yes, at the core of your BEingness
You feel the Creation Aligning within

Two Souls coming together IN full Unity
On all time frames and dimensions
For the world to shine and BE free
IN Love with no shame or guilt

When they appear, you will know
This is what you have prepared for
For this Divine Union
To Feel One with all

Anticipate the Ecstasy
Of all you ever dreamed of
And every ancestor before you
Even Gods get to experience the pleasure
Of the Love between the two of you

Your Love becomes a gift to all
For all that is and ever was
For the One with everything
And nothing at all...

Pure Bliss and Ecstasy
Your high hearts become One
Unifying the field to inspire
The world to Choose Love

This will BE a Love
Healing all the gaps
Created from the battles
Before this Union has come

They will feel familiar to you
As if you are looking in the mirror
How can this BE true?
It pulls you IN to BE home with you

They feel home yet, a different mystery
Something you don't have, yet long
New Codes that will unlock
When the two of you meet

Oh, what an Exhilaration you Feel
Get comfortable with this Divine Love
So, you know the power that can drive
The world to appear right IN front

BE ready to Unite
With the mirror IN front of you
IN flesh with powerful chemistry
They will BE One with you

Energy Vortex

The road you take is simple
The mind will complicate all things
The colors begin to Create
With the entire energy field

Think, when you have another person
Being near you
The energy Connection between the two
Will form a Vortex
It might feel tight, neutral or good
Depending on the Frequency held

If you connect two bodies
That are not Aligned
With their heart and Soul
With no life force to Love

The energy vortex will BE absent
To Create or Evolve anything
That is possible between two beings
Connected to Heart and Soul to Feel

We are quantum Creators
We are beyond what we See
That is how we can explain
This vortex of Energy

Ready To Meet?

This is a Love like no other
Are you ready for it?
They are coming towards you
Rushing ahead to meet

They just received a message
From the Spirit, of who you are
They begin to INnerstand
Their attraction thus far

The intensity of the pull
Is igniting their Heart
To taste the Ecstasy
Of being with the ONE

The Stars are Aligning
All begins to make Sense
The veil is being lifted
And they can See again

The memory is flooding
With scenes from the past
The Love of Eternity
That you both forgot

They remember your Love
They remember who you are
They remember your Soul
They have come so far

They have endured it all
Lies and manipulation
Searching for something real
The ideal IN co-Creation

Now, they know
How could this BE real
Their Dream person
Has appeared material

They Remember you
They are Calling for you
The intensity of this Energy
Will wake you up from sleep

They need to BE near you
They are hearing the call
The Spirit is Awakening
The DNA path for you

Know they have the Wisdom
They have the Source within
They remember their Mission
To come IN Union with you

Chapter 11 - Sacred Union

Surrender To Union

One sees the other
And can no longer unsee
The reaction of the body
To their entire field

The other hears the Voice
And feels something Awake
Something dormant before,
Now becomes Familiar to feel

Both parties Feel the pull
As if you heard the calling
To Unite for something more

Than a simple beginning

Your hearts are beating faster
You begin to imagine the Dance
The Love making intensity
In One dream of Embrace

You are called towards each other
To Embrace all that is new
The life as you knew it
No longer holds true

You long for each other dearly
You know the intense power it holds
You lose control of your thoughts
Your body feels Ecstatic once more

What is this sensation?
How do you explain this pull

How can you long so deeply
For One you haven't met before?

The intensity is real
You both can no longer ignore
This is a call at Soul level
To Unite once more

Surrender to the intensity
They will respond to you
Like an Open Lotus flower
As you share the loving pull

BE One with this sensation
Your Soul knows what to do
You have designed this path
It will make Sense to you
Let go and follow the pull

First Contact

They are reaching out to you
IN dreams Searching for you
Asking for a Sign,
On how to approach you

The Desire is deep
They can lose control
They have One shot
To make this Union work

How could it BE?
Searching an entire life for One
And now, seeing it before your Eyes
There is One shot to make this right?

Before the tides pull
And they must wait...
For another Opportunity
Could BE weeks or lifetimes

The pressure is on
If they can have a sign from you
If they knew for sure that, is you
Or do they?

They will find a way, they have to
The entire Universe is conspiring
To make this Union come true
BE patient and ready to Receive
The One for you...

You Know

You know the Feeling
Shifting you from the inside
You could BE miles apart yet, sensing
As if you are here, side by side

How can you Feel another so deep
How can you Hear their thoughts
How can you Sense their Desire for you
Are they aware that you know this too?

Who cares at this point?
This intensity is out of your control
Your Soul is Awakening you to come close
To feel them near, even if across the World

So far, yet so near
As if they are here with you
Embracing IN loving Ecstasy
The One meant for you

Can you Feel their Heart and Soul
Deeply craving you?
Hear their roar,
It will Awaken you

What is this riddle
What am I preparing for
How Intense can this get
What kind of Love is this?

It seems out of this world
How can I long so deeply?
For a person I haven't met before
What is this entire riddle?

How can I take a break
How long will this last?
It's moving me IN motion
To lose all train of thought

What is this Connection?
I thought, I was Ready for
If it feels so strong apart,
What would I Feel near them?

Is this to get Ready?
To Feel such pleasure to BE
Simply knowing of each other
Oh my! How intense can this BE?

This is a powerful force
A Love out of this world
As if the Gods themselves are plotting
To experience this Love through me

Is this the Highest Love?
Meeting each other at God level
That explains the intensity,
Even miles apart...

I will Feel it and Surrender,
This is the only choice I have
I have called upon this Love,
To Feel the ecstasy of Gods on earth

I surrender to this pleasure
With no interfering thoughts
No more questions your Honor
I am IN Love with Love!!!

https://channelingevolution.com/join

Chapter 12 - Manifest Union

Call Them IN

Call your Lover IN
It is time to Connect
On the physical level
So, you can Manifest

Call them with your thought
That you are ready for connection
Open up your Heart
To Feel the powerful Vibration

Feel the body Open
Like a lotus Flower
Receive the luxury
Of this Love power

Receive the energy incoming
Of the person you dreamed to BE
Feel the nourishing dance of two beings
IN ecstatic weaving of Sacred Energy

Call them with your readiness
To trust this Dance to BE
Receive the instinct of shifts
Needed to make space within

The Reason

The reason for this Union
Will come to you as a surprise
It has been Prophesied by masters
That the New World will arrive

You attempted for centuries
To Connect your twin flame Love
Entangling even more
IN the karmic contracts

You have transcended this level
The Twin had the chance to revive
You have attempted this riddle
For several lifetimes

The One Union you search for
Is more Powerful than that
It's not a mirror perse
But the opposite part of the spectrum

They will BE your match in Power
Not exactly the same suit
It will BE a reflection of other power
To Create the New World for good

This is not just a Union
Between two searching Souls
It is a Union between all beings
And all nations around the World

Get ready for this Union
It will defy all that you know
It would BE the utmost perfection
Of the other side of the coin

Embrace Love Story

Love story, embrace me
With your Luxurious wave
Lift me in a Vortex
Of pleasure in Divine way

Love is the Easy part
Love with no limitation
Pain comes from the ego
Imposing Love suppression

This is the Love power
To transcend all illusion
Allowing the flow of infinite God
To transmute mental confusion

Love story, show me the way
To Connect with my reflection
To dance IN a Wave
Of this powerful expression

Love story, quench my thirst
With the drops of Eternity
Feed my hunger to experience
The Nirvana of this Serenity

https://channelingevolution.com/join

Chapter 13 - Against All Odds

Interference

There can BE interference
IN a sense that you know
And on the energetic level
Of the opposite forces of flow

BE prepared for the battle
Simply BE at Peace...
IN the middle of chaos
Know that leads to this

The love story you are calling
Will shift many lives to come
Therefor interferences
Are placed to stop this

Make no mistake, you won
It is only a matter of Alignment
All is shifting on your behalf
BE happy and joyful in your garden

Focus solely on your Joy
And the world you came to build
BE happy and the rest will find you
When they are ready

A Taste of Home

A taste of Home is calling
Whispering sweet words of Love
Embracing you IN its Energy
Full expansion of the Heart

Oh, what a peaceful feeling
To BE so wholly, here, now
Kissing the sensation of Divinity
You Surrender to the Highest path

Oh, a sigh of such relief
It felt like a forever walk
Searching for that Home
Now, found IN our Heart

Home sweet Home, I'm here!
It has been so long...
I thought my home was out there
I had left my Throne

Oh, it's so good to BE here
To Remember the now
That I belong here
That I'm Home at last

Home delicious comfort
And Fire to Expand my Heart
The water quenching my thirst
While I travel the Universe

Hold me dear Home
Like you would hold a child
Allow me to traverse life's challenges
With utmost Ease and Grace

I Love you my sweet Home
I will always BE Present, here
I had traveled the entire world
To realize that my Home is here

Sweet Home thank you for waiting
So patiently for me to arrive
Like a Loving Mother awaits
For her child to come home at last

Love Portal

Enter the Love Portal
And never look back
It will Guide you towards each other
Surrender to the instinct you Feel

Allow the Guidance
And follow the subtle nudge
The Universe is collaborating
For all parts to Align

Do your part by being Present
So, you can Hear the call
When guided to follow a thread
Do it with no Question at all

Enter the Love Portal
Imagine this bobble of Light
Containing the God Codes
For the two of you to Unite

Feel its Light energy
Expanding your Field
Keeping you in Ecstasy
Of this upcoming heat

Wear the bobble daily
It will Guide you through
It will Create the Path
That is Aligned with you

https://channelingevolution.com/join

Chapter 14 - And so, it is

Clear Doubt

What do you believe
Stands IN the way of this?
What do you believe to BE true
Write it down and clear the way

Burn the paper
To erase that possibility
And Imagine the One
That feels right to you

If you find the cause externally
Look IN the mirror, for now

Ask, how is this belief
Helping my story unfold?

Change the narrative to adjust
And all the doors will Open
For you to experience
The Love you came to

You both want the same thing
And the only thing that stops it
Is the belief that something else
Needs to happen before it happens

Let go of all expectations
All beliefs that stand in the way
Clear the entire trajectory
From illusion of values
We hold so great

Union Contract

This Love story
Has been Written by you
By your Desire to experience
A Love out of this World true

You saw that IN your Vision
You seek a Love like never before
No One has showed you the possibility
Yet, you are here searching for...

You know deep inside
That you have signed a contract
To meet IN this lifetime
And experience what is possible

You have agreed to Meet
To Recognize each other
Creating a new Love story
That will collapse 3D reality

This Love will BE like no other
A fire roaring through your DNA
A Vision that takes over
Your Path of night and day

You longed for this Union
It's the One you searched for
Because you came to make it real
And experience Heaven on Earth today

Bathe IN Love

Bathe IN the frequency of Love
The highest pleasure you can imagine
Open up your Heart and Feel
The Ecstasy of Union expression

You are dreaming of each other
You can even Feel the Touch
You begin to converse telepathically
As if they were there, by your side

Bathe IN this Dynamic
You will get to know a lot
It will bring to the surface
All that needs to BE placed aside

You will get to know each other
Mentally, before you even meet
You are getting ready to Align
With the personality IN 3D

At the Soul level
The alignment is set
Now merge that Connection
To Align IN the 3D realm

Go through this dynamic
And when you find a block
Anything that stops the Connection
Alchemize it IN your Heart

Get ready until there are no more "buts"
When you are ready to jump IN
Get your suitcase ready
To fly when the Universe says, let's begin

Chapter 14 - Silence

Feeling The Other

I feel so much

Frustration at the core

Why am I longing for a Love

That I haven't felt before?

A longing for another

To meet me at such dept

To hold space for all of me

The same way I can BE

Is there another?

That matches my desire to Love

That can INnerstant the waves

Flowing through my Heart?

Why do I Feel the longing?

When I am this person for me

Why do I feel that there is another

IN this world that matches me

I had made peace

To BE all of that for me

To Love and meet myself

To the level satisfying to me

Why search the world for another
If another hasn't shown to exist?
Why do I Feel that there is a match
Made in Heaven on earth to persist?

Why such deep longing?
When I have all I need, inside
Why long for a match?
That I haven't found outside

Is there truly another
That can meet me at my dept?
Is there another searching for me
So, we can finally Connect?

There must BE another...
Or the longing won't make Sense
I am at peace and IN Love with me
I give myself all that I need

Why this longing burns so Deep
Why the Desire wakes me up
Why Feel another so close
Like they walk a parallel side?

Is this a part of the riddle?
The quest I must embark on again
Or will I sit on my throne?
And allow the other to appear

The answer has been spoken
I searched the whole world before
Until I found what I was looking for
Deep inside of me...

Yet, the dream is shouting launder
There is another that has been born
A match to BE by my side
To walk this path along

I will sit on my throne
Sovereign IN who I am
I will embrace this Desire
And simply allow it to Manifest

If there is another being

That can connect with me IN form

It will Magnetize to my path

And meet me at my Dept

I Feel the burning sensation

Running through my veins

The deep longing for Connection

I have not met IN this world

I know this is real, it has to BE

It's been a vision since I was a child

A person who truly knows me

And we can See each other

It feels like we walking

Parallel realities

Getting to know each other

IN all dimensions, but 3D reality

I will allow the Feeling

To show me the real Truth

If another was born to BE with me

From the Allness, it will appear to See

Union Questions

More questions arise
"When will this happen?"
Let go of time and you will know
That they are already here

Don’t rush the process
If you don’t See them yet
Unplug from the illusion
That it must BE a certain way

Simply BE ready
And know that it would happen
When you let go of the idea
That there is anything else you need

Look IN the mirror and See
That you have already arrived
The One you have searched for
Is looking IN your Eyes

Love this BEing here
And know for sure that One day
The outer world would mirror
Your Ecstasy withIN

You Are Feeling

You are feeling the Surrender
To what is coming near
Don’t get attached to Timing
And push it ahead my dear

It will happen when it's time
When you truly let go...
Of the idea how it happens
When you will Unite IN home

Let go and you will land near
As if the Stars knew all along
It will find you Loving dear
Let go and Surrender, to loving you

https://channelingevolution.com/join

Chapter 16 - Sexual Energy

Sexual Energy

Your Sexual Energy
Is already spoken for
They have spotted your Presence
IN the 3D world

You will Feel the heat of Desire
You might wake up IN sweats
The arousal will envelop you
When they crave your essence

Embrace this anergy and allow it to Rise
To turn you on with every breath
Rise it to your Crown chakra
And wear it with pride

Bring this sexual Energy
Up the spine with heat
Swirl it IN your body
Like a vortex of energy

Let it Rise to your Crown
And release it at the top
For your Light body
To absorb its sight

This Light body is your shield
To hold such Union Energy
You will both develop this skill
Your Sexual energy is Currency

BE IN Desire

Harmonize with the Love Sound
By transporting your very self
To the most Luxurious place
Your Soul longs to experience

BE there now, envelop in all senses
See the Beauty you came to See
Breathe IN the air of this Heaven
Feel it embracing your Home to Feel

Smell the scent of fresh air
Flowing through your Chosen place
Taste the Joy of your inner Child
Receiving all that it needs

Rest in the Luxury of this moment
It is the best of here... now
Feel the Sensation of living
The most Exhilarating life!

Hear the Sound of life
Vibrating through your body
Feel your Heart aligned with Love
Receiving the here now moment

Transcending Time and Space
You are Experiencing all of this
Traveling to your Dream place
While here, reading this

What is Real and what isn't?
The questions cease to exist
Only the mind can stop this unfolding
You are already together, IN the Universe

You are here, and IN every desired place
You are alone, and with your Lover
Connected to the entire world
Let go and experience it all!

Ecstasy

Experience the Luxury
Of touching each other
Let your Body explore
Every part of the other

Allow yourself to Open
Before it comes to BE
Feel the intensity of what
This unfolding could Feel

Explore the Pleasure of Union
Feel it's exhilarating embrace
Forgetting where you end
And the other begins

Your bodies become One
Enveloped in a Vortex of fire
The third Energy intensifies
The potency of each Desire

You breathe each other as One
Hearing the moans with intensity
IN fact, the sounds of your bodies
No longer need permission to BE

The heat is expanding the Heart
Beyond its human capacity
The Source from within
Is exploring Ecstasy

https://channelingevolution.com/join

Chapter 17 - Created Reality

Recognition

At the crisp of a dawn
You will know who they are
As if wishing on a Star
You can See this far

The realms are Connecting
For the 3D worlds to Unite
Yours, theirs and the third,
You will Create this time

You have done this before
It is a repeated Story
You continue with Grace
You already have the victory

You are simply repeating what you know
The long-forgotten Future
You came back to paint the Picture
And show examples of it all

Your Path is Unique to you
You both had opposite beginnings
They are the other side of the coin
The One that has been looking for you

They have searched for you, in others
Finding small pieces here and there
Believing that if they place them together
They can Create a whole being, here

They have gathered pieces from the matrix
From relationships with all
From all that others are searching for
Yet, still looking for someone...

It is you, they are looking for
And nothing else can fill that void
You have been looking for them too
Searching the entire World through

You are merging your Worlds
Beginning in opposite sides
You will meet IN the middle
To BE in Union at last

Your Union is the Prophecy
Of uniting everything to BE
Your Love plays a role of Creation
IN the New Earth to See

Created Story

This story is being created
Right here, IN real time
Yes, with your Highest self
With your utmost Divine

You are creating the story
By Opening up to more
Allowing the God in you
To write your own Code

You are creating your future
Into the Divine matrix reality
As you Focus your energy
On this possible reality

You have the power IN your hands
While illusion tries to distract you
With fear and made-up problems
Induced by the collective thought

You both have the ability to quiet
And listen with your Heart and Soul
Allow the hearts to open like two flowers
Uniting as they become One

You had just plugged into
Divine Union power

Their Perspective

From your lover's perspective
You have no idea,
How much you're asking for
The bar seems so high
Like they are not able
To reach it no more

And they will BE correct
It is a wall, no One can climb
Yet, only the right partner
Will have the Key to enter the sight

They See you as a puzzle
A Code impossible to crack
The closer they come to an answer
The more questions arise to ask

They are faced with a dilemma
Feeling that the price is high
Yet, their whole beingness
Can't imagine living another way

They can no longer conform
To what felt good before
They are willing to lose it all
Just to BE with you

They See you as a prize
But not the kind you think
The One their Soul is searching for
The only way back home from Dream

They See no other way
But to walk with you
No life they lived before
Will make sense without you

They are ready for you
They simply don't know what to do
They grasp the power of control
To forge ahead towards you

https://channelingevolution.com/join

Chapter 18 - Aligned Desire

I Feel Them

Why Feel such power?
That will shatter all beliefs
Restoring from inside out
The infinite power of Bliss

Why Open up?
To such Vulnerability
And what choice do I have
To resist the intensity of this Love?

I Feel it IN my Heart
I Feel it IN my bones
I Feel my mind letting go
Of all that stands IN the way

I Surrender to this Pleasure
It is beyond my power to control
This is the Soul Destiny calling
To become One with all

I Feel all gamut of Sensations
No longer holding onto any truth
This Love has no boundaries
Or labels, that can contain its Bliss

It is the true Godly power
Strength and intensity, I longed for
It is the Chemistry, Joy and Wisdom
All in One being Evolved

They are right here,
I can feel them, hear them
I can taste the flavor of their lips
Caressing every part of my tender skin

I hear the beat of their Heart
Sinking in One rhythm with mine
I Feel the longing of their body
To BE near mine...

I Feel the intensity
As if they are One with me
What is this Magical experience
Who is the One dreaming with me?

Open The Flower

The flower of life is unfolding
Opening up your Heart field
As if a Higher intensity Energy
Joined you on this Path to succeed

Your walk, Feels like flying
Minutes apart, Feel like years
Miles apart are unbearable to imagine
The Connection is here to Feel

Feel them near you
As they can Feel you too
Simply embrace each other
Connect for your Highest good

Feel the comfort of this Wave
As if time and space had stopped
IN the Ecstasy of every moment
Nothing can keep you apart!

Allow the Love of this moment
To remind you why you came
Feel the Divine Eternity
Upgrading your DNA

You become them
And they become you
When you come close
IN heart forming a Unity

Allow yourself to Feel them
They are as tender as you
Longing for the same Love
You Feel inside of you

It is safe to BE here

It is safe to Allow

The One you hold so dear

To BE a part of you

Higher Love Portal

Enter the Love Portal
From a new perspective
From the Godly self
Or Master, if it feels better

Step into Highest side of you
And from that Godly level
Connect to the One
You are meant to

Feel the Highest you
Embracing the other
Helping to Harmonize
The codes between each other

Your highest selves will Unite
All parts of you, on all levels
Simply Open up your field
To experience it on 3D level

Connect from Goddess to God
Honor each other from that level
Coronate each other
And embrace the equal Godly level

This is what Divine Union will call for
To See each other in your highest form
To Honor the God in each other
And continue the Path on

https://channelingevolution.com/join

Chapter 19 - Embrace Duality

Yin and Yen

This is the duality
You are invited to Embrace,
Attachment to spirit or material world
After experiencing each One of them

What if you didn't have to Choose
What if there was no light without dark
No Beginning without an end
No Resurrection without death

When you begin to cease
Holding on to any side as good
You will simply Dance to the music
IN the expression of the Highest Truth

You are invited to Master both
Marrying the spirit and material world
Dancing in Tantra of light and dark
The Highest expression of Unity

For this Divine Union to come to BE
Fear of choosing wrong will cease to exist
When you Embrace the Duality within
IN Unity you will BE free to See

Hot And Cold

Hot and cold is the expression
Of this Union, coming to BE
Breaking through all the constrictions
That were there before to See

Your field needs to BE Open
To receive all that is coming through
You have carried the cross before
Now is your time to Receive

Hot is your Highest self-transmuting
All that stands IN the way
Cold is the fear trying to put out the flame
Staying stagnant with what you know

Hot and cold will Play around
Until you learn to simply Observe
Heat will cool off, as you know
That you are, already IN Union

Cold is what you know
It is the victory of the small ego
Yet, you have tasted the freedom to BE all
IN dance with the past and future

While being so Present with all
No rushing, or even waiting
Simply Feel IN Union, now
What if they are here already?

Feel your Happy ever after
Feel that inside of you
You are IN Union with you
And you'll always BE here for you

Because you are, eternally you
You are One with all around
Therefore, already in Union
Feel the sensation of home

Being IN Divine Union
Breathe and enjoy the inner peace
Laying IN each other's arms
Dancing IN One breath t Fee

Hot and cold, IN Harmony
Dance with the gamut of all that is
In One tantric Connection
Of sweet loving Union
You deserve this

Change

The walls are shattering
So many parts of your life fade away
You can Feel their energy intensely
So much doesn't make sense this way

It feels as if they are here
You Feel their life melting away
All that needs to dissipate
For this Union to BE on its way

The timelines are shifting
They are being prepared for you
As you have done it willingly
Now, you can hold space for both of you

Everything is shifting
You feel every part of this journey
It wakes you up at night
It takes over your body

They need your support
You are the only thing that makes sense
They have seen the illusion
They have lived before

Their life is shattering
And you can Feel it all
You are prepared for this
IN the 5th dimension, you are whole

BE patient and hold the line
Of the Highest timeline
Allow the feelings to flow through
Dance your Heart and shine

They will come to you
Shine bright your Light
So, they can See ahead
While forging towards you

Shine your Pure Heart
And express the Highest you
Only at that level
They will truly know, it's you

BE in bliss and Joy
Alchemize what comes to you
Dance the energies away
As they flow through you

Your Peace and Joy, at this point
Will speed up the Union
The more you are IN Alignment
The faster it will Manifest before you

Chapter 20 - Higher Level Union

4D Connection

Love, BE here, now
Feel them as if they are near
They are next to you know
Sense their Light body

You begin to live a life IN 4D
Supporting each other telepathically
Through all that you already know
As you get closer IN 3D

Allow this Love story to unfold
As it begun on the Soul level
Now moved to the mind
You can hear them
As if they are here

Engage and get to know each other
Transmute all that comes from the past
Get Aligned IN the 4th dimension
So, you can BE ready for the 3D life

They will speak and laugh with you
They will make Love to you
They will keep you up at night
They are what you've been asking for
Receive and get to know you

This part is important
Different than you have been thought
Through the 4th dimension
You get to transmute the trauma
So, you can BE free to Love
When you Connect IN 3D life

You are doing the work before hand
You are getting to know each other
You are becoming familiar with you
Sharing stories for Alignment

All this happens, before you meet
So, you can BE fully Present!!!
When you meet IN 3D reality,
You will BE ready to Love
With no holding back

Take as long as you need, IN this transition
Until your bodies crave each other nonstop
And the mind had lost its grip
Of all the possible confusion

When you are Whole and have no fear
When you are ready to take that leap
4th dimension Activation will integrate
So, you can finally meet

You left an imprint on their Heart
The moment they had seen you
No longer will they BE able to envision
A life without you IN it

They will Rise to the occasion
And the Temple you have built
No One has been able to climb
Because it takes a special key

They key is not a word
Or a specific action
It is the actual being
That was meant to unlock it

They will BE the key
And your Heart will Open
You will no longer See
The fear of illusion
You will BE ready to come
With them IN full Unity

You Are Ready

You are Ready now
Because you no longer care
You had fully focused
On your life's trajectory

What you longed before
You had found inside of you
You Feel at Peace fully being
IN Love with all you are and do

You had made peace with the story
You had found access to all inside
You are fully, here
And Love is your birthright

You realize that what you longed for
Was for another to mirror to you
The Love that you already are
But could not See IN you

You can give yourself that intensity
And Love yourself, as deeply as you do
You are your own match
You have achieved Divine Union

Initiation Complete

This Initiation is complete
You have done your part
You integrated the Codes
Now you can move on

You received the codes for a story
Of the Kingdom spouse to BE
The Universe has your openness
And will act on your behalf to See

There is nothing you can do
IN fact, you are asked to let it go
To focus fully on you,
And your Happiness!

The more you think about Union
After you integrated the Codes
The more you elongate the time
You are asked, to fully let go

Trust the Creator IN you
That you have all that you need
BE in Divine Union with you
And the rest will Magnetize to you

About The Author

Veronica Parks

Welcome to the Soul family

Beautiful child of Light

Veronica Parks comes to you as a Channel

To share the Awakening codes from Divine

Veronica was born in a 3rd world country

From eastern Europe side

She had grown up IN control and poverty

Even abuse didn't miss her Path

Veronica is a Warrior
Paving her own path towards Love
Aligned with the Soul Healing journey
To heal her own Heart

Through her path she has created
Guiding many others along
She is the founder of "Angels Gate Academy"
A path to heal the Soul

Now she is called to Channel
The awakening IN form of Poems
To share with the world
Her expression of the Code

Veronica Parks is a being
Just like you, having experienced life
She is equipped to take you on a journey
To Awaken the Divine Union Love

✨Connect✨

Thank you for Connecting

With lovers IN mission

Please continue the journey with us

Through the avenues below

YouTube-

https://www.youtube.com/@ChannelingEvolution

Join Channeling Evolution Family -

https://channelingevolution.com/join

Angels Gate Academy-

https://mastersoulhealer.com/join

1st Book of Channeling Evolution-

https://www.amazon.com/dp/1968682015

2st Book of Channeling Evolution-

https://www.amazon.com/dp/196868204X

🩶 Review Request 🩶

Please take a moment

To share a Heart review

It will help more Divine Unions

To receive these messages too!!!

www.ingramcontent.com/pod-product-compliance
Lightning Source LLC
LaVergne TN
LVHW010915110826
845149LV00013B/2374

* 9 7 8 1 9 6 8 6 8 2 0 2 6 *